POEMS IN AN EXHIBITION

An Anthology of Poems Inspired by Art

In support of Standing Voice

AN OXFORDFOLIO PUBLICATION

Standing Voice

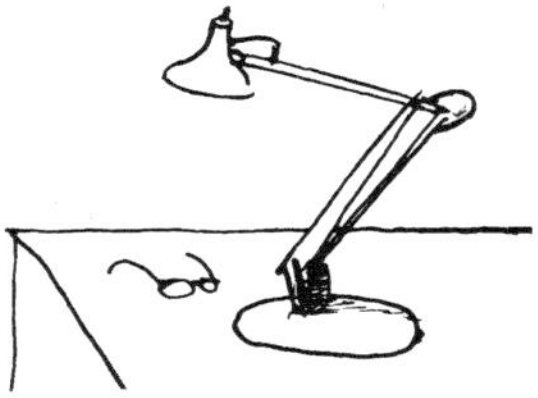

An OXFORDFOLIO Book
46 Hayfield Road, Oxford, 0X2 6TU
www.oxfordfolio.co.uk

Design and typesetting: Philip Hind
www.philiphind.com

The author and publisher wish to thank the poets and artists, art galleries, museums and publishers for permission to reproduce the poems, paintings, artefacts and photographs in this book.

Printed by Latimer Trend

ISBN: 978-0-9956794-3-6

British Library Cataloguing-in-Publication Data

A catalogue record for this book is available from the British Library

10 9 8 7 6 5 4 3 2 1

Detail from *The Weston Library through the Clarendon Building*
© Weimin He, 2014.
Inside front and back cover, p4 and 45 photo credits: Harry Freeland / Imogen Freeland / Chihiro Tagata Fujii / Standing Voice

CONTENTS

THE STORY BEHIND POEMS IN AN EXHIBITION

TOLD BY SYLVIA VETTA

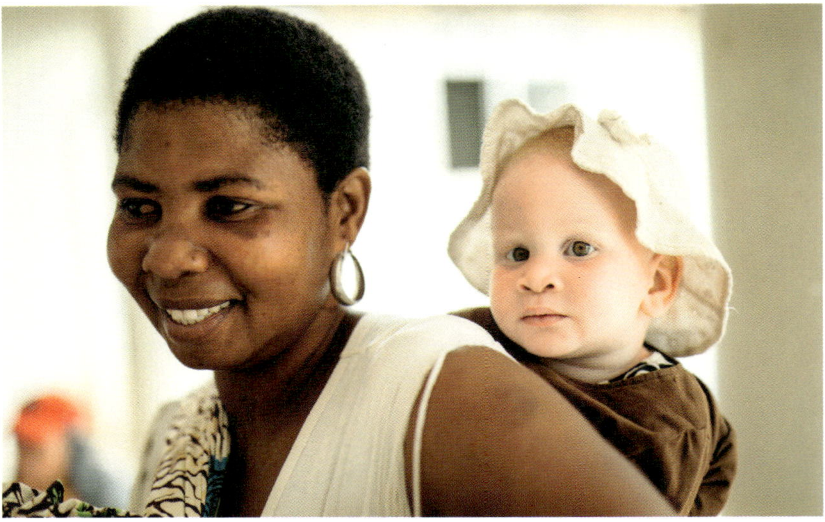

Standing Voice exists to end human rights abuses against marginalised people. My village of Kennington (Oxfordshire) has for 49 years fundraised for development projects. Our intention has been to help people help themselves. Each January KOA chose, by vote, one out of three projects. In 2015 we invited a relatively new charity—Standing Voice—to submit a project.

Award-winning British documentary filmmaker Harry Freeland spent six years in Tanzania documenting the marginalisation of people with albinism. During that time he made *In the Shadow of the Sun*, a film that told the story of their courage in the face of persecution. The film inspired the founding of Standing Voice, a human rights charity that helps people with albinism to claim their rights and stand up against stigma. Standing Voice's programmes—in Health, Education, Community Development and Advocacy—are designed to empower and be replicable. We were impressed and chose them for the KOA 2015 project funding a skin care clinic to prevent cancer. At that time people with albinism were dying of preventable skin cancer before they were 35. We were equally impressed by the delivery of the project, which has since been replicated in Malawi funded by the Malawian government. (see Standing Voice: Who We Are & What We Do, pp 45–47).

WHY POEMS IN AN EXHIBITION?

In February 2017, the BBC broadcast a documentary made by the Standing Voice team and titled *Born Too White*. Halfway through this moving film we were introduced to Festo. Aged 7, Festo was badly mutilated with a machete, his teeth and fingers taken for sale to a witch doctor. When the film was made Festo was nine and an inspiration. Using his remaining thumb and a piece of nifty surgery creating one finger, he had become a talented artist. I told his story to an artist friend Weimin He. We decided to send art materials to Festo and his friends, and Weimin wrote a beautiful letter from one artist to another, and sent Festo a painting especially for him. That painting inspired me to write the last poem in this anthology *Born Too White*. I am passionate about art and for ten years I reviewed exhibitions for *The Oxford Times*. I love poetry too but only seem to write poems in some way triggered by works of art. Hence the title of this anthology!

I approached some mostly Oxford based poets to contribute to this anthology. The idea is that all proceeds from direct sales will go to Standing Voice for the art summer school they run on the island of Ukerewe in the training centre built by Standing Voice. Young people with and without albinism will enjoy art together forming friendships and changing attitudes.

I hope readers will enjoy these poems and consider writing one. I have opened the anthology with one of mine. I felt we should have a gallery for our poems and pictures, and one I love—being half Cornish—is Tate St Ives.

ACKNOWLEDGEMENTS

Thanks to all the poets and artists who have given their work free of charge for publication in this anthology.

Thanks to James Harrison of Oxfordfolio and Philip Hind for producing this beautiful book.

I would also like to thank all the people in Kennington who have supported KOA during its 50 years of fundraising.

My personal thanks to Jenny Lewis who as a teacher on Oxford University Continuing Education's Diploma in Creative Writing gave me the confidence to believe I could write a poem worth sharing.

Thanks to all purchasers of *Poems in an Exhibition* for supporting the charity Standing Voice.

Sylvia Vetta

THE POETS

Simon Altmann
Penny Boxall
Arabella Currie
Euton Daley
Dwina Gibb
Jenny Lewis
Shakira Morar
David Olsen
Heather Rosser
Adnan al-Sayegh
Sudeep Sen
Sylvia Vetta

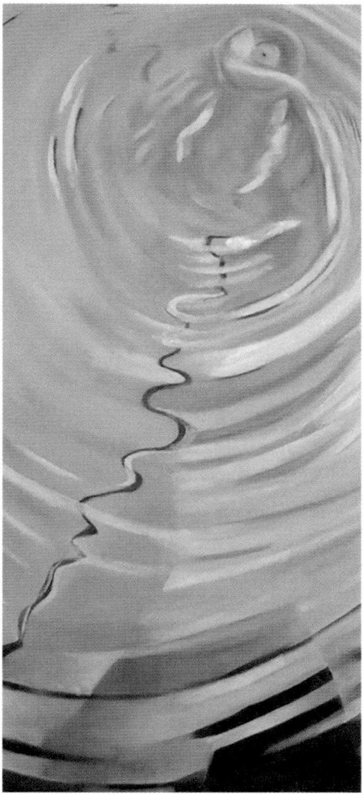

THE ARTISTS

Weimin He
Naz Perver Weich

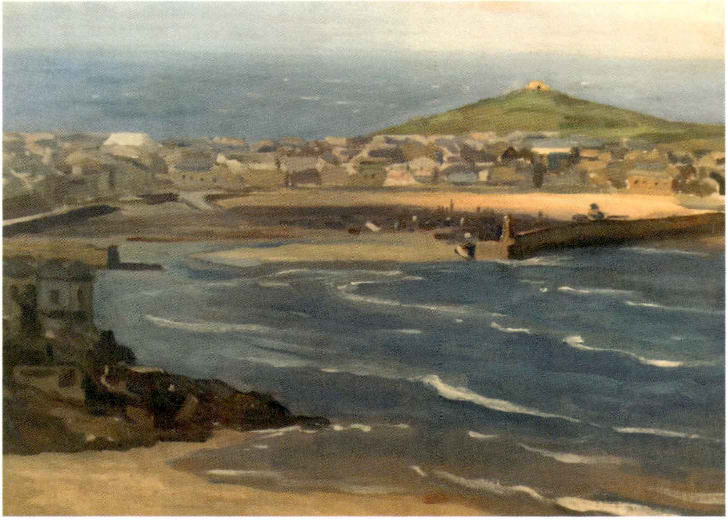

St Ives Bay
Marjorie Mostyn (1893–1979)
By kind permission, Joanna Harrison

TATE ST IVES

BY SYLVIA VETTA

See Peter Lanyon's headland rugged
and Nicolson abstracted, Hepworth's stone
smoothed by the wash of time.

Sea and sky framed; painted
within the window above Porthmeor beach
Below, sand, pebble and speckled shell.

Surf froths gently over baby's toes.
She held safe as father's eyes focus
inland as the sun sinks behind granite.

Faint in the distance from Cornish land comes
clay wheeled by the hand of Bernard Leach,
as, startled, Patrick's heron emerges with a fish.

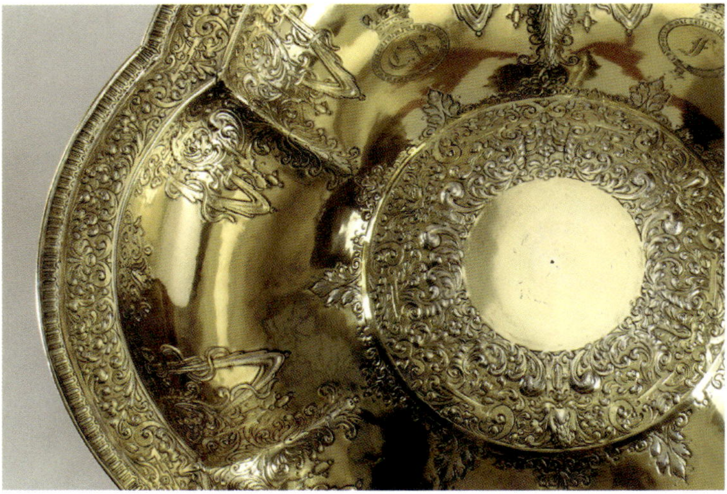

The Rosewater Basin
London, 1616/17, Silver with later gilding
© The Holburne Museum

THE ROSEWATER BASIN

BY JENNY LEWIS

What's on his mind as he hammers
the silver, makes light flower
        from beaten metal?

That line of low hills, clouds in the dips
and hollows between stretches
        of water still as a mirror,

might have the king's name on it
        under a sky seared by the smoke of forges
just like this one.

And beyond London, the world, New England,
bigger spaces, prairies, unknown lands
        mapped by totems –

their gift to us was turkeys, ours
        to them, disease
   and decimation:

like us they ate with knives and hands,
        no forks, and washed themselves
in rain and rivers

while we used scented water, our shared residue
        of grease and spit masked by the smell of roses
from the apothecary's garden.

The Rosewater Basin by Jenny Lewis originally published in From Palette to Pen, *an anthology of poetry and art edited by Frances-Anne King for the Holburne Museum, Bath, 2016.*

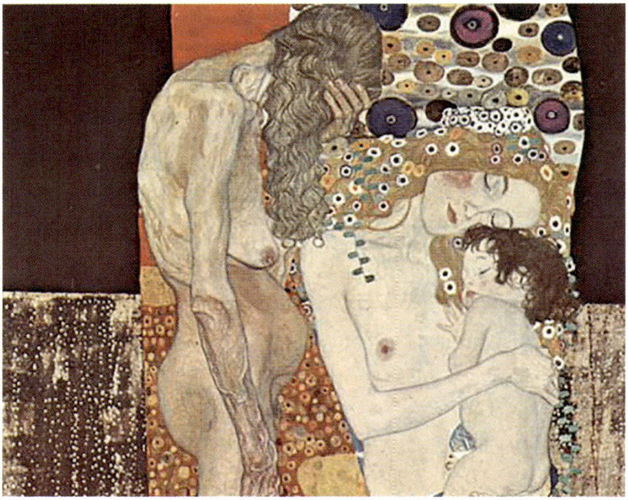

The Three Ages of Women
Gustav Klimt (1862–1918)
Wikimedia Commons

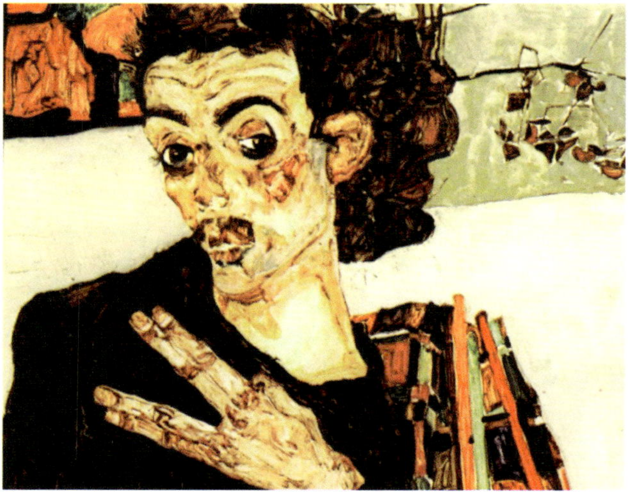

Self Portrait
Egon Schiele (1890–1918)
Wikimedia Commons

HANDS

BY SIMON ALTMANN

Klimt's hands are not hands
for strength. Comfortable and concave
they are designed to accommodate
to a cosy backside or to quietly test
how gravity may be suspended
from a friendly breast.

Schiele's hands are not hands to touch,
except perhaps pen or brush.
They are raucous manifestos
that need not stretch
to unfriendly skies to protest
their alienation from the world around.

Not this for Klimt: let his hands
lie quietly on a lap ignoring
the hardness and anguish of life.
They are not hands to grope and despair,
to search, to find, to strive
and never to home to a habitat.

That was Schiele's task.

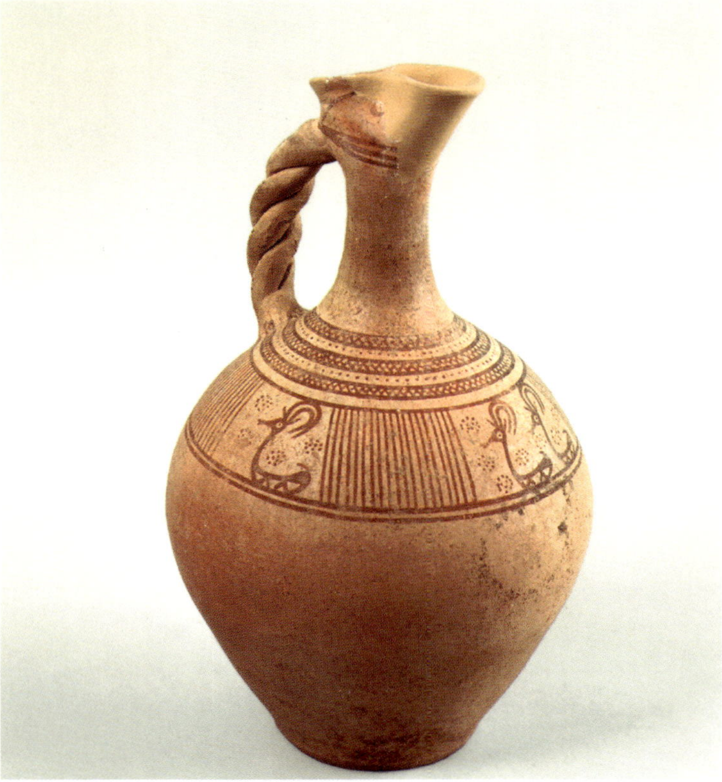

THE CRACKED JUG

BY SHAKIRA MORAR

The girl dips her jug into the river,
Whoosh goes the water.
Sweet thoughts are her friends.

She lifts the jug and embraces it,
As a mother with her baby would.
The drops are her lifeline.

Carrying the jug, she takes many steps
To find herself in her home.
The four clay walls are her shield.

She pours the water for her brothers,
Gripping the handle tightly.
Those drops are their lifeline.

Her mother lifts the jug
To set on the shelf, next to the stove.
Her mother preserves their lifeline.

Her father returns from work,
Concern pulling him from the present.
Her father reveals her reality.

Her earth shakes with terror,
The jug topples to the ground.
The crack foreshadows her fate.

Clay shards cut her face.
The girl pulls herself from the rubble.
Stinging thoughts are her enemies.

Winner of the Poetry Society's Poetry for Peace Prize, 2016

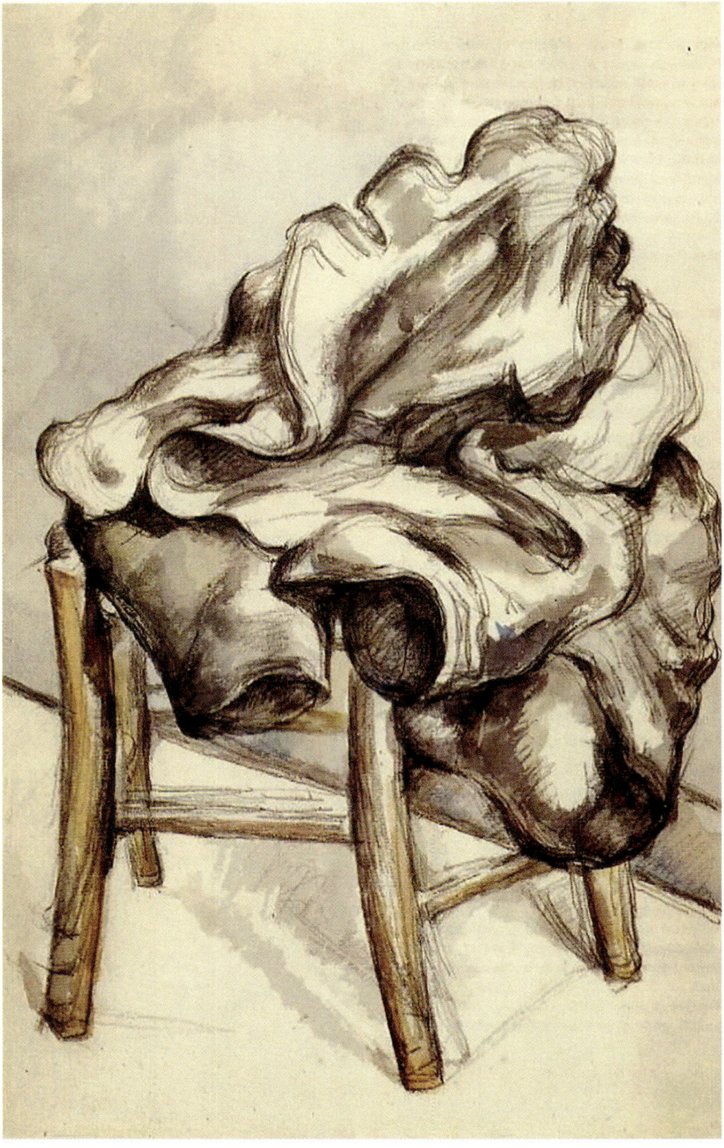

Jacket on a Chair
Paul Cezanne (1839–1906)
Wikimedia Commons

JACKET ON A CHAIR

BY SUDEEP SEN

You carelessly tossed
  the jacket on a chair.
The assembly of cloth

  collapsed in slow motion
into a heap of cotton —
  cotton freshly picked

from the fields —
  like flesh
without a spine.

  The chair's wooden
frame provided a brief
  skeleton,

but it wasn't enough
  to renew the coat's
shape, the body's

  prior strength,
or the muscle
  to hold its own.

When one peels off
  one's outer skin,
it is difficult

  to hide
the true nature of
  blood.

Wood, wool, stitches,
  and joints —
an epitaph

  of a cardplayer's
shuffle,
  and the history

of my dark faith.

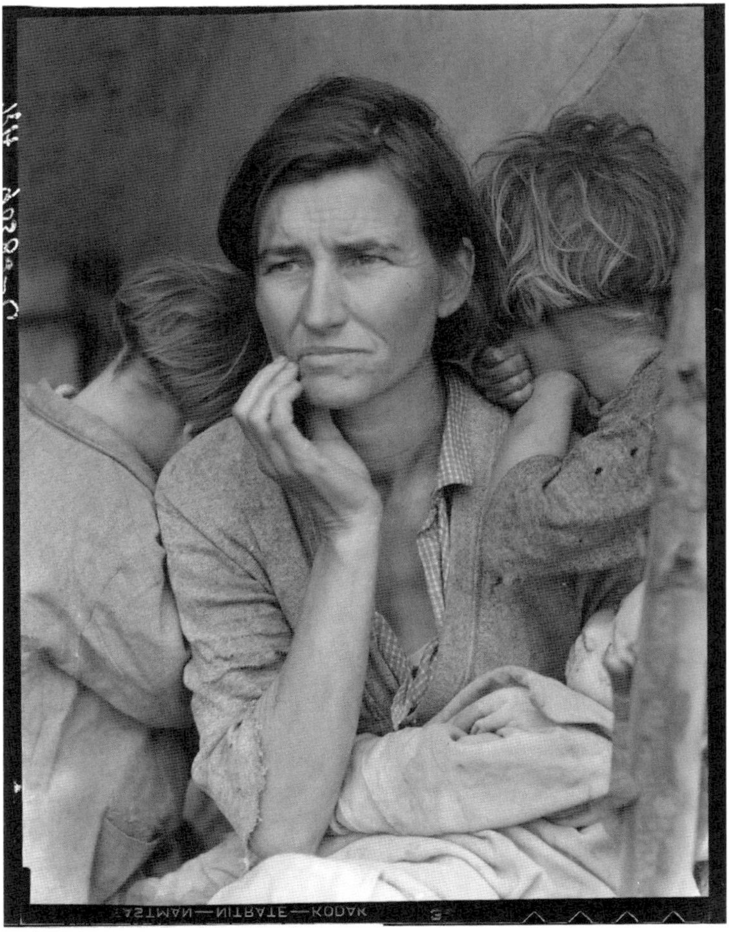

THE MIGRANT MOTHER
Dorothea Lange (1895–1966)

THE MIGRANT MOTHER

BY DAVID OLSEN

They huddle in a slumping soggy tent
in an uprooted pea-pickers' camp.
Caught in mid-squirm, two grubby boys
avert their bewildered too-old gaze.
Too weary for play, another sleeps
on mother's lap. Everywoman's eyes
scan a furrowed horizon of care.
She strokes her fretful face with slender
fingers worthy of diamonds.

Foreclosed, busted in the dust of Arkansas,
deceived by bills that promised farming work
(in a glutted market that ensured
the lowest wage), they came in a juddering
jalopy laden with the frayed remnants
from the bolt-ends of dignity.

Her car boiled over in mountain passes
and coughed across that unforgiving desert.
She sold the tyres for food, and survived
on vegetables pilfered from nearby fields.
Enduring intrusion into private strife,
she hopes the picture in *Life* might summon help
from somewhere beyond this harvest of shame.

Dry winds and drought were less to blame
for the rent fabric of fiscal failure
than bankers addicted to the heroin
of too much easy money.

Now, like burrowed moles – complacent,
overfed and over-borrowed – we drowse,
blind to the spark of the diamondback's
tongue, asleep to the chill of the fang.

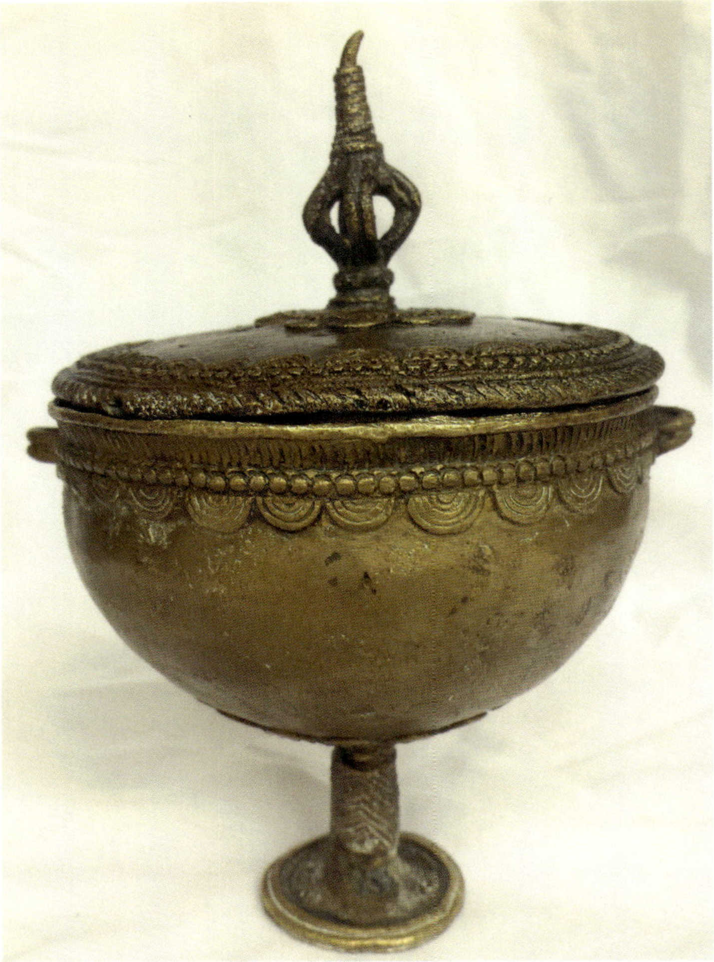

The bronze chalice was given to Heather when she was living in the Mandara Mountains of Nigeria.

THE BRONZE CHALICE

BY HEATHER ROSSER

Sitting cross-legged on his grass mat the Blacksmith
Chips away the clay mould with infinite care.
Squatting beside him, his Grandson watches
Mesmerised, as glimpses of bronze are revealed.

Oblivious to the sun's heat, swishing of tall grasses
And murmuring of women's voices as they pass
Balancing pots on their heads,
The Old Man painstakingly continues his work.

All afternoon the Boy watches, creeping closer,
Spellbound as an exquisite bronze chalice is revealed.
Cupping it in his hands the Grandfather
Solemnly gives it, his final creation, to the Boy.

His eyes widen as he gazes at the
Intricate carvings around the rim and the
Tiny pillar on which the chalice stands.
'I will keep this forever,' he whispers.

The Old Man shakes his head.
'Cherish it well till the time is right
To let the spirits within it pass to another place
As I will soon pass on to join our ancestors.'

Many moons later in the City of Oxford
A story-teller delves into his Box of Things
And holds up the chalice
For eager children to imagine its story.

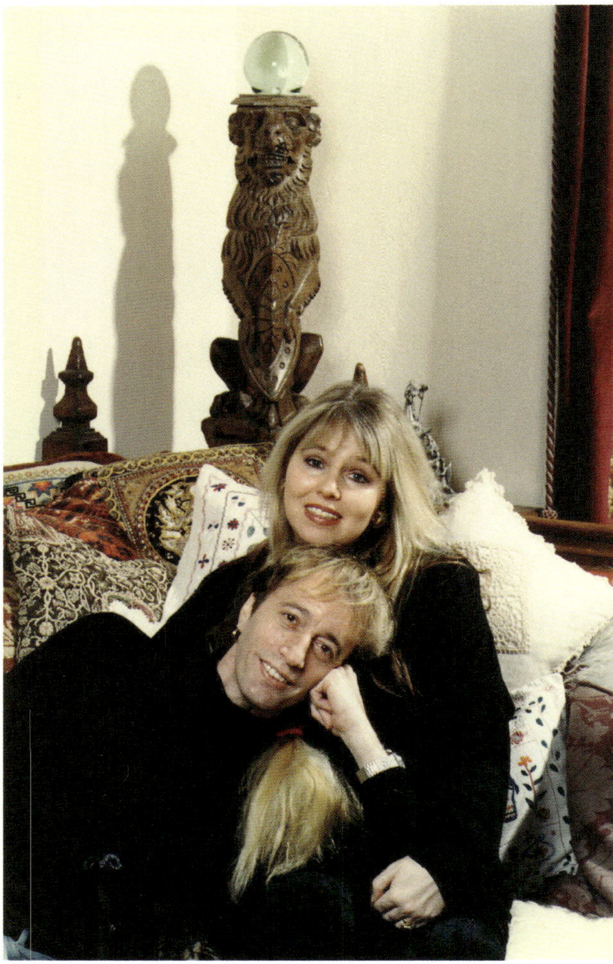

ROBIN AND DWINA GIBB
© Dwina Gibb, by kind permission

MY SONGBIRD HAS FLOWN

BY DWINA GIBB

My songbird has flown and the world sighs
The gentle mouthpiece of his immortal muse has gone
And no music can be heard that is sweeter than the language of his love
No diamond is more precious than the memory of the twinkling in his eyes
And no treasure in the lands will replace his happy smile.

My songbird has flown and the world sighs
And if I were to paint a third of what I feel
A masterpiece would be yours to have and hold and hang upon your wall
If I were to write the words that spill from my heart
Tomes and volumes would make your library wide and tall
If I were to sing songs of praise for him
Saints would rise to make a chorus fit to please angel heralds
And if I were to make music for his gentle ear Celestial
harmonies would dance in all the worlds.

And so no more, his voice now stilled but never gone
A depth of silence reigns where once he had his say
The veil of night has fallen
But a dawn of the Divine will rise for a new day
My songbird has flown and the world sighs
But we know that he is never far away.

Dwina Gibb : For Robin, my love, my life

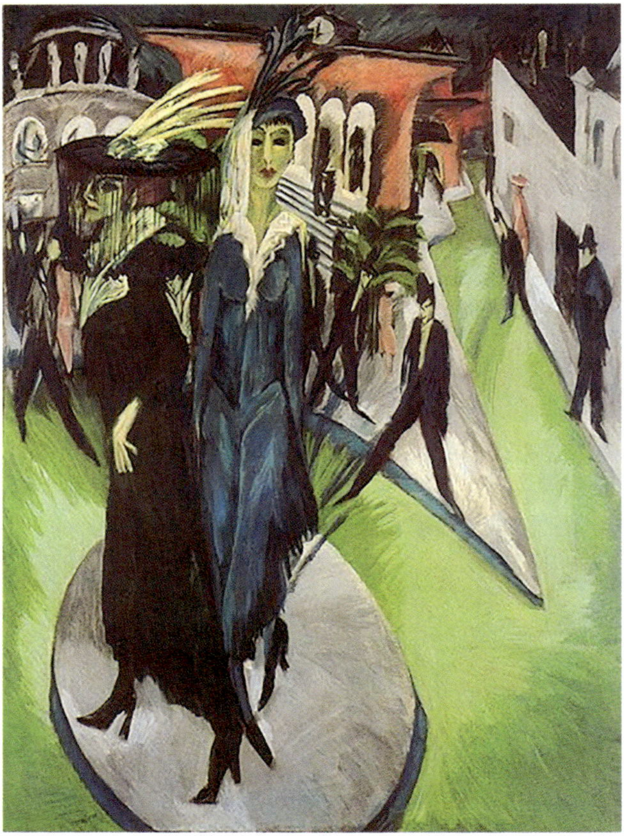

Potsdamer Platz
Ernst Ludwig Kirchner (1880–1938)
Wikimedia Commons

POTSDAMER PLATZ

BY SIMON ALTMANN

Two gigantic figures in elegant dresses
and huge hats: ladies of the night.
Scattered punters, waiting, observing.

A huge wedge of brick and mortar,
now faithfully replaced
by the same shape in steel and glass.
That was the square, that is the square.

No more ladies waiting now:
motorcars dominate.
The magnificent tension of the picture,
like a stretched bow ready to discharge
its arrow, is now gone.

But then the painter used
the wedge of the building
like an ominous axe threatening
the desirable pleasures of life.

Degenerate art, so was this called
by a great country
and so was proscribed.

This was soon accompanied
by the greatest crime
ever committed by humans to humans.

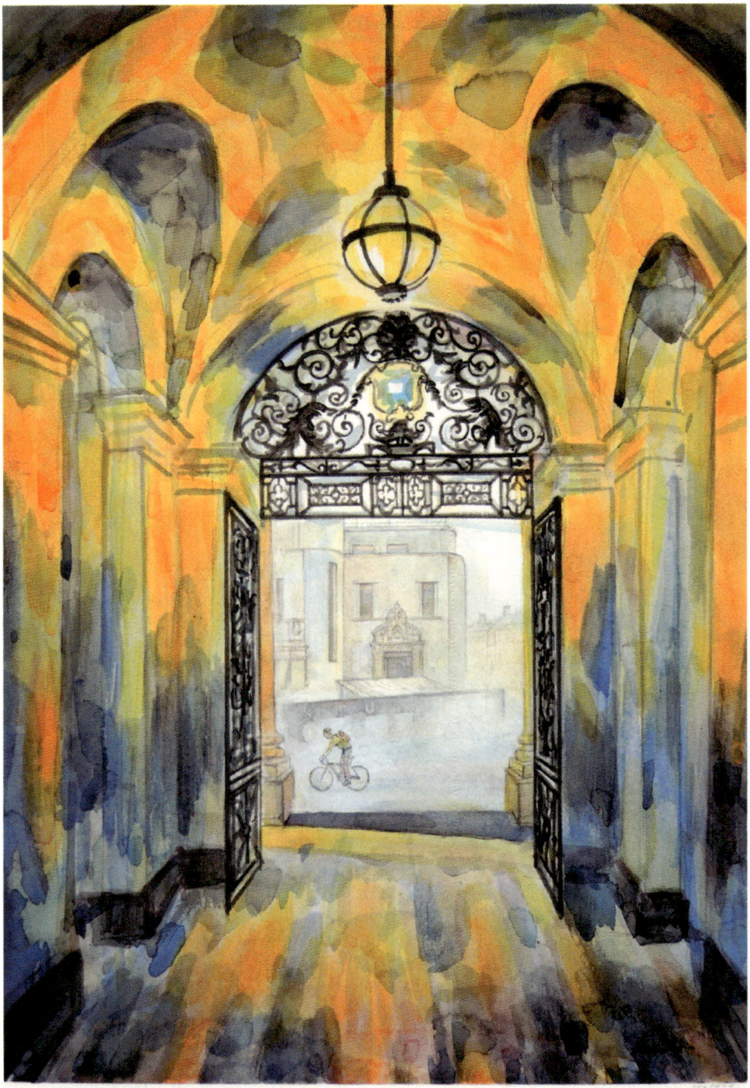

The Weston Library through the Clarendon Building
The work is created for the Oxford University Estate Services Art Project

THE MISTS OF DAO

BY SYLVIA VETTA

Memories of Shanbei come in shades of black and white.
Amid the stones of Oxford past and present he paints it.
I reach out to touch it, real but not concrete.
Celtic mists swirl in with rain from the West
to shower the East, clouded in the spirit of the Dao, and meet
in the mind of the artist. Fingers grasp the brush to request
the muses for movement, swift and light.
Brushstrokes colour the paper red with his spirit.
His being connects time and his energy fires
a gateway to the here and now, and clear
ahead cranes point skyward with the dreaming spires.
Visions of a future beyond hard lines appear.
To the music of a new time in a new place
The artist walks alone into the white space.

道之雾

陕北的记忆渐入黑白光影。
在牛津的碎石之间，过去与现在由他笔绘。
我伸手触摸，真实而非具体。
凯尔特的薄雾交缠着雨露，自西而来
沐浴着东方，笼罩着道之精魂，相遇
在艺术家的观念之中。弄指握笔请愿
来吧，灵动、轻捷与明亮的缪斯。
灵魂的笔触将画纸渲红。
他的画意链接了时空，他的能量之火
开通了时与空的大门，
抬头仰望，依着梦想的塔尖。
未来之景在坚定的线条中浮现。
在别处的新时光的乐响之中
艺术家独自走进了纯白空间。

First published in The Madras Courier *(2017)*
Chinese translation by Yang Xiaoya (Zhejiang University)

FIRST LIGHT

BY ARABELLA CURRIE

What we thought was full of shoals
is a shoal itself – its torn, silver-backed filaments
slack in the breeze.
Water brushes water,
itching to be first to reach the end.

All over the surface
uplifts pick themselves up by the pore
and push on. Sunlight

idles between air and landing
but the sea just spars
and leapfrogs under.

Cormorant dive by cormorant dive,
breasting its way –

to where? To more water? To open water?
To land? To berth?

The sea is going somewhere.

And now you're on it.
Walking on water.
Light-stepping to some island
of the blessed, some windward island,

somewhere far from all those worlds
you lifted anchor from.

Where
apprentice swimmers

dip their fingers
in the stream
and feel for movement.

Where we know,
now,
that when these rucks and ripples
stop, it's water arriving,
it's you
running over dry land.

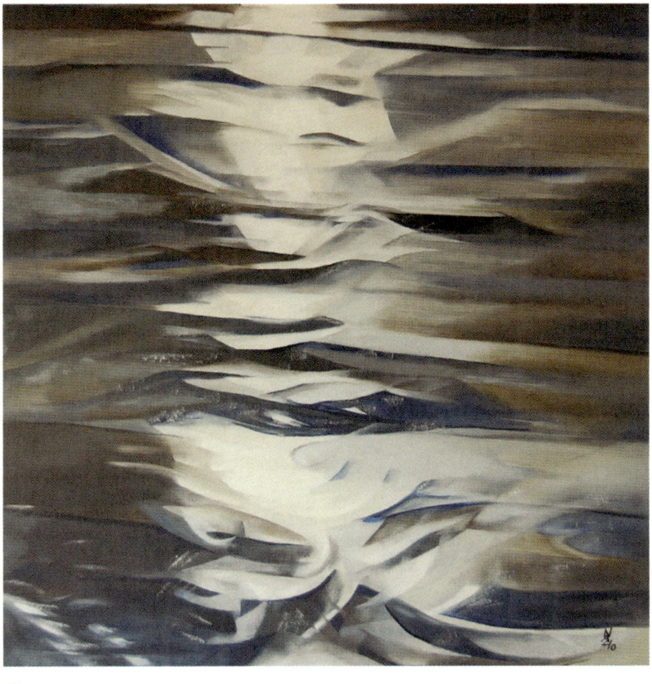

First Light

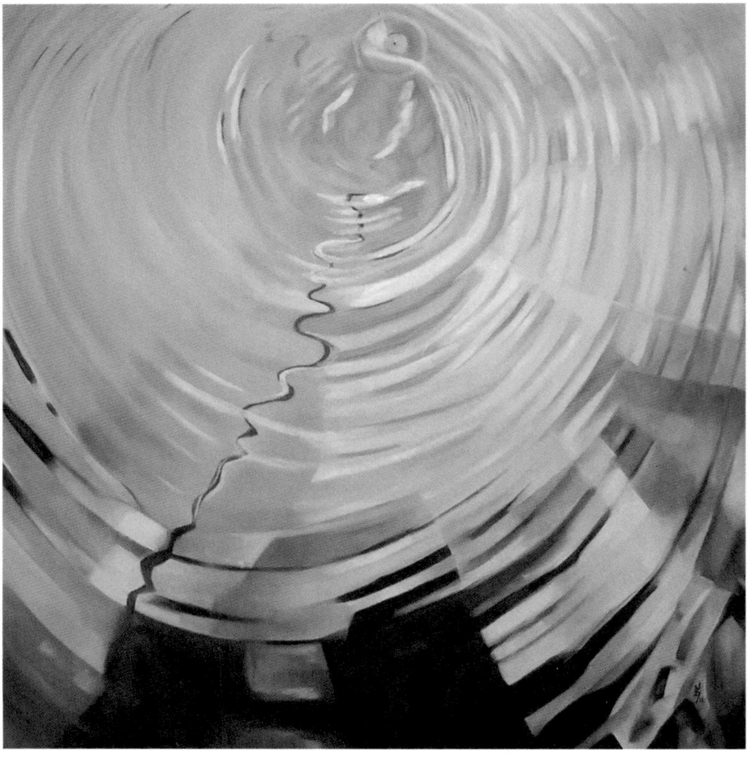

Ripples

THE WHEELWRIGHTS

BY PENNY BOXALL

The clock, of course.
Mum drying a bowl
with a blue-and-white cloth.

The breeze muscling in
on wet hair. Water
evacuating via
the plughole or,

to put it another way,
down the plughole
in Australia.

Mistaking white noise
for your name.

A helicopter from above.
A helicopter from below.

The earth on its axis.
Tumbleweed.
You mid-
cartwheel, seeing it through

until the world
has righted itself again.

IN EMERGENCY—BREAK GLASS

BY EUTON DALEY

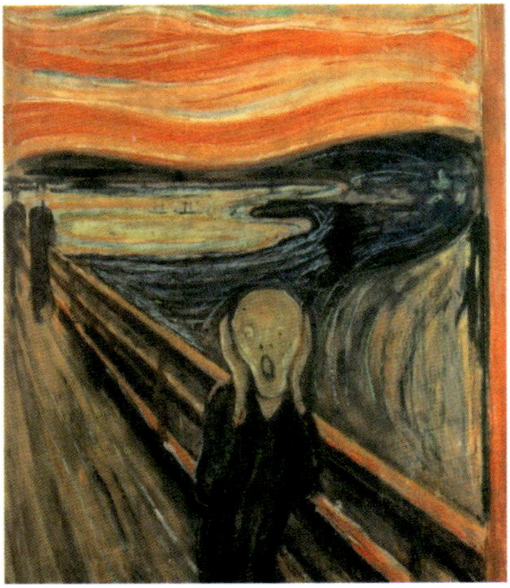

THE SCREAM
Edvard Munch (1863–1944)
Wikimedia Commons

Close your eyes

Close your eyes
Close your eyes
Take a deep breath
Think
Make yourself invisible
Think!
Ho-ho hold
Hold the anger back.

Hold the anger back
Not in shame
I have nothing to hide
But out of fear
You hold the anger back
Just, just
hold the anger back
Ho-ho hold
Hold the anger back

Hold the anger back
A say, hold the anger back
It's not a question of right or
wrong
You just
Hold the anger back
Stop. Think
Take a deep breath
No more tears to be shed
No more blood flow from these
veins
Ho-ho hold
Hold the anger back
Hold the anger back

This poem is the first part of a poem for performance

When the rude boys attack
For the umpteenth time
And you scream for the
umpteenth time
And the neighbours
Behind their net curtain barricades
Choose not to hear
Or just don't care
And the passer-bys
Don't stop, call for help
Nor mutter placating words
You just
Hold the anger back
When the institutions
Conceive to block each and
every avenues

And everyone accepts
That's the way of the world
And when you cry to your friends
And their only sympathy
Is to let out a sigh
You just
Hold the anger back
Yes, hold the anger back

When the colour of one's skin
Is your identity badge
You want to shout
I'm not just a colour
I have a name
And my name is
My name is
My name is
Hold the anger back
Hold the anger back

Ho-ho hold
Hold the anger back
Don't be intimidated
They mustn't have the privilege
Don't show the hurt
Or the hatred
That you feel inside
Hold the anger back
With dignity
Hold the anger back
It mustn't be allowed to eat you up
Let it give you new strength
With each and every blow
Take a deep breath
Bide your time
Hold the anger back
Just, just hold the anger back
Hold the anger back
Yes, yes, yes, hold the anger back
Hold the anger back

Warning: In Emergency—break glass

[Screams – long and piercing]

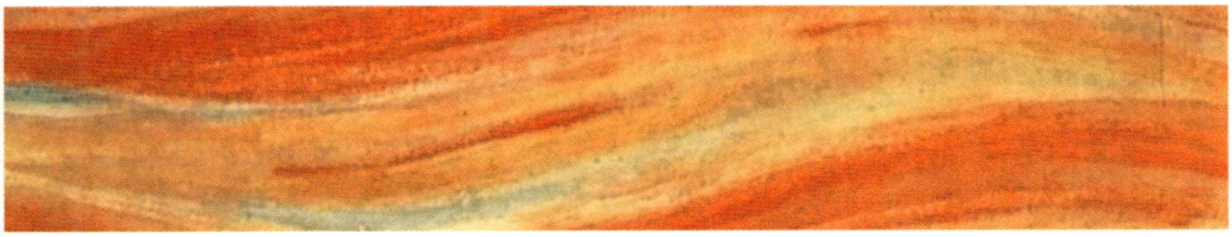

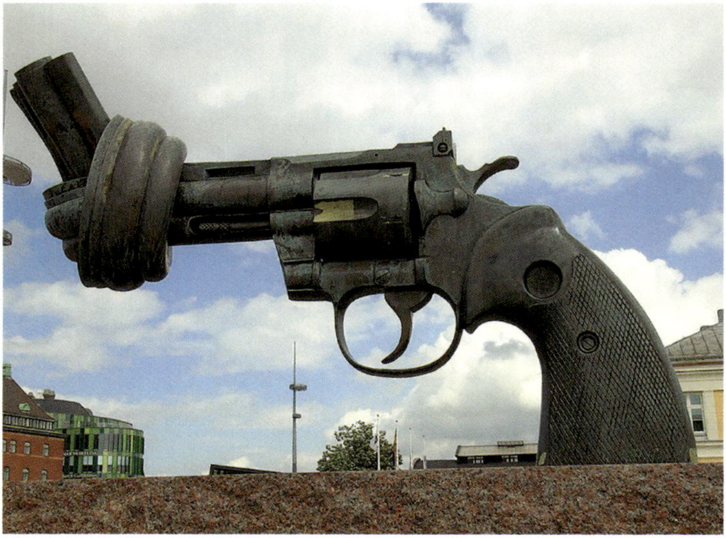

NON-VIOLENCE
Carl Fredrik Reuterswärd (1934–2016)
Wikimedia Commons

EXTRACT FROM URUK'S ANTHEM

BY ADNAN AL-SAYEGH

TRANSLATED BY JENNY LEWIS AND RUBA ABUGHAIDA

I open the album
   and cry for friends who died in the night of the battlefields,
for the cities, the memories…
why does the war shatter me in two?
   Why does night stamp on my chest like a soldier's boot?

I try to write in darkness – stealing light from flares:
The bombardment began heavily tonight,
   shaking us like sardines in a can.
         We are not dead or alive:
And (…I was born, and died…)
And (…no mules or soldiers killed, no losses or gains…)

News bulletins make us switch to other frequencies
which crisscross the stony trench
carrying scum and capital cities in miniskirts, wars,
   mass murder, exiled revolutionaries, an advert for a
platonic, chocolate-flavoured aphrodisiac.

And tomorrow, who knows where we will be buried?
We who have no hand-span of land and can own no grave or
shroud.

(The American bulldozers bury us, far away in the desert,
then the wild animals dig us up, so our families bury us
again, then the bulldozers of the Republican Guard dig us up,
then we are buried by the…)

First published in Long Poem Magazine 15, 2016

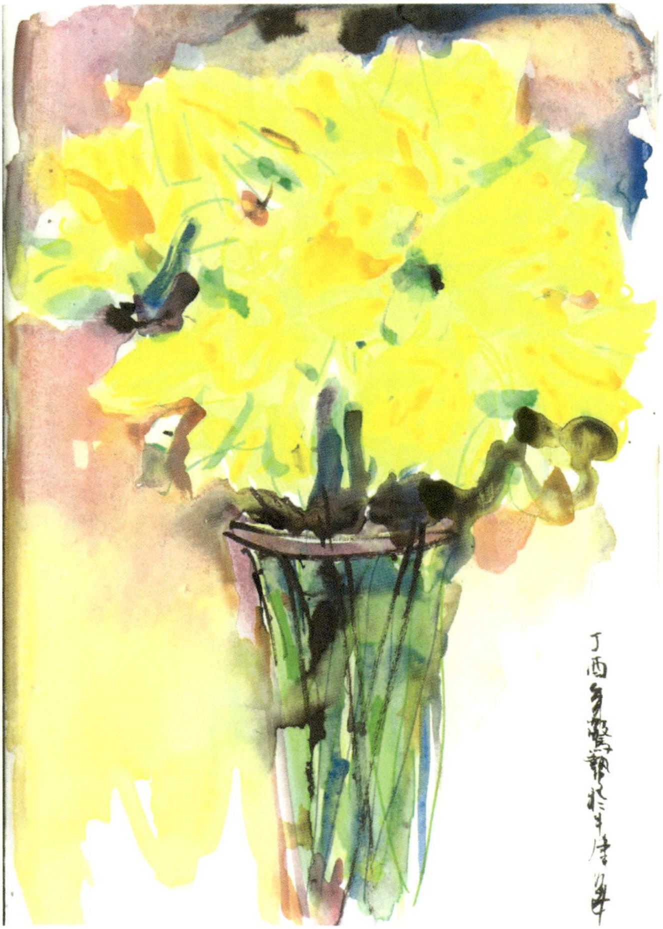

FLOWERS

BORN TOO WHITE

BY SYLVIA VETTA

His neighbours label him as other - not black like them -
but 'Albino'.
Men of cruelty and hate rob him of teeth and fingers.
Body parts sold to 'medicine' men who greedy for gain,
feed the superstitions of powerful politicians.
His courageous spirit defied the blade.
Beyond survival, Festo flourishes.
His inner self blossoms to paint and draw.
From the frozen north of Manchuria
an artist recognised a fellow artist.
Weimin painted for Festo a vase of glowing flowers:
harbingers of Spring and hope.
No need for translation.
Festo's spirit, not too white
but in vivid colour.

ABOUT THE POETS

Every poet like every human being is unique and has a unique voice but this collection has unusual diversity. Some of the poets are famous and extensively published and others are just starting out. The youngest poet is 18 and the oldest is 93. They come from 4 continents although all now either live in or often visit the city of Oxford.

SIMON LEONARDO ALTMANN

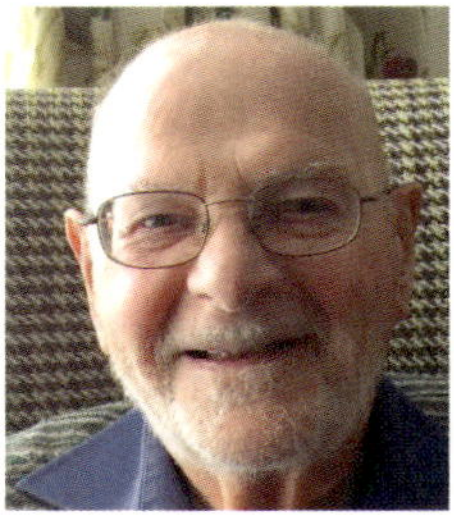

Simon Altmann was born in Buenos Aires in 1924 and became a mathematical physicist whose main work has been on group theory, quaternions, and solid state. Simon started out as Lecturer in the Theory of Metals in 1959 and in 1964 became Fellow and Lecturer in Mathematical Physics at Brasenose College. In 1991 Professor Altmann became Vice Principal and then retired as an Emeritus Fellow of the College. Since his retirement his main interests have been history and philosophy of science, poetry, especially science poetry, and some work on art theory, mainly concerning right-left problems.

ARABELLA CURRIE

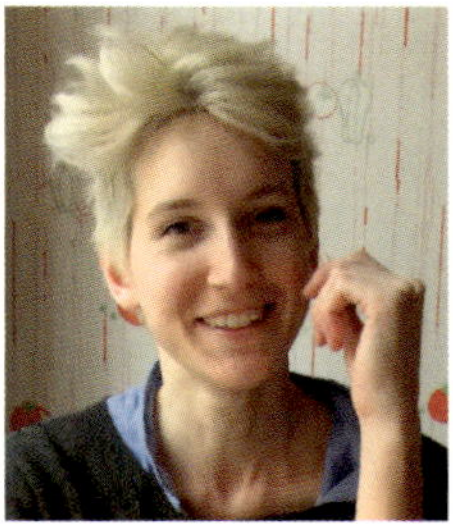

Arabella Currie recently completed a DPhil in Classics at Oxford, about the interrelation of Greek and Celtic antiquity, and is now working on a new project about William Golding and the Classics. She published her first poetry collection, *The Divers*, with Hurst Street Press in 2016. Her poems have won various awards, including Oxford's Newdigate Prize, and she has translated several Greek tragedies for the stage.

PENNY BOXALL

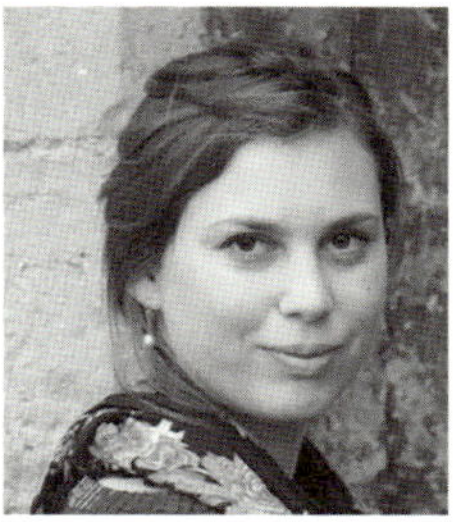

Penny holds an MA with distinction in Creative Writing (Poetry) from UEA. Her collection, *Ship of the Line*, was published in 2014. She won the 2016 Edwin Morgan Poetry Award. She is a 2017 Writer in Residence at Gladstone's Library and Hawthornden Fellow. She won first prize in 2016's Elmet Poetry Competition and second in the 2014 Jane Martin Poetry Prize. Her poetry has appeared in various publications, including *The Sunday Times, Rialto, The Forward Book of Poetry 2015, The Salt Book of Younger Poets, Magma, The Literateur, Mslexia,* and *The North.* She was formerly an Associate Lecturer in Poetry at Oxford Brookes. Penny is currently Heritage Education and Volunteers Officer, University Church of St Mary the Virgin.

EUTON DALEY MBE

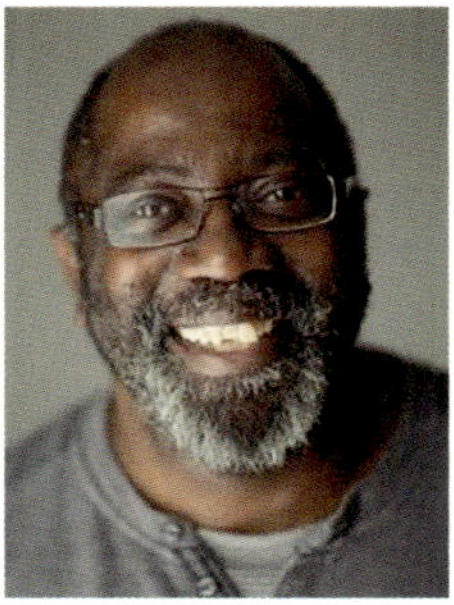

Working as producer, performer, writer, director and tutor, Euton is totally committed to using the arts as a tool for expression, exploration, communication and entertainment.

He founded the *Unlock the Chains* Collective in 1986 to explore performance poetry as a theatrical form. It reformed in 2013 when Euton left Oxford's Pegasus Theatre after 23 years as Artistic Director and CEO, to explore and present black experience and culture and to give Black artists a performance platform. His poetry book+CD, *Politics of Love*, (Ackhi Press), was produced in 2015 and his next collection, *Ending the Silence* will be out in early 2018. www.eutondaley.com

DWINA GIBB

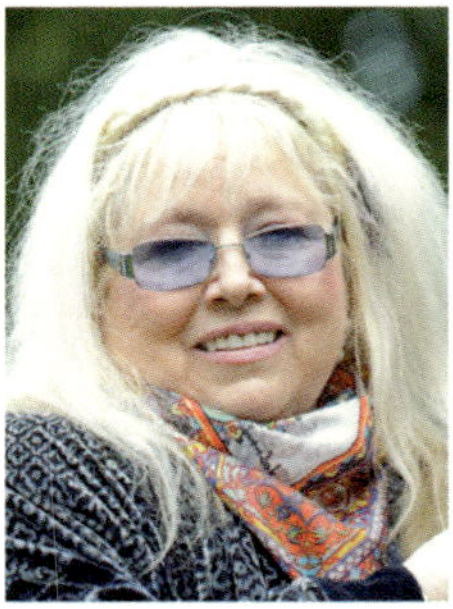

Irish-born artist, poet and playwright Dwina Gibb was the co-founder of the Yeats Club and published Celtic Dawn the International literary magazine. She has published two volumes of poetry: *Ergot On The Rye* and *Butterflies and Drums* (under the penname of Bridie Morrigan), and her third collection *Love Abound* is also available on CD. Dwina was much influenced by Seamus Heaney who she met at a poetry workshop at the Yeats Society in Sligo '... he admired my poem *Mullaghmore* particularly "pinched hoof prints"' she recalls. Dwina was married to Robin Gibb of the Bee Gees and her poem tells poignantly of 'his voice now stilled but never gone'.

JENNY LEWIS

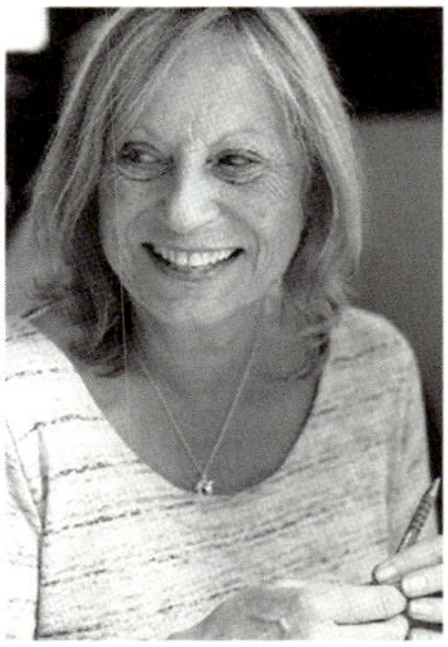

A poet, playwright and songwriter specialising in cross-arts collaborations of poetry, music, dance and visual art, Jenny Lewis has published three collections of poetry: *When I Became an Amazon* (Iron Press, 1996/ Bilingua, Russia 2002) *Fathom* and *Taking Mesopotamia* (Oxford Poets/ Carcanet 2007/ 2014) and three chapbooks from Mulfran Press in English and Arabic with the Iraqi poet, Adnan Al-Sayegh – *Now as Then: Mesopotamia-Iraq* (2013), *Singing for Inanna* (2014) and *The Flood* (2017). Her poems have been published by leading journals including the *Cork Literary Review*, the *Financial Times*, *Poetry London*, *PN Review* and *World Literature Today*. Jenny's latest work, *Gilgamesh Retold,* is forthcoming from Carcanet Press in 2018. She teaches poetry at Oxford University.

SHAKIRA MORAR

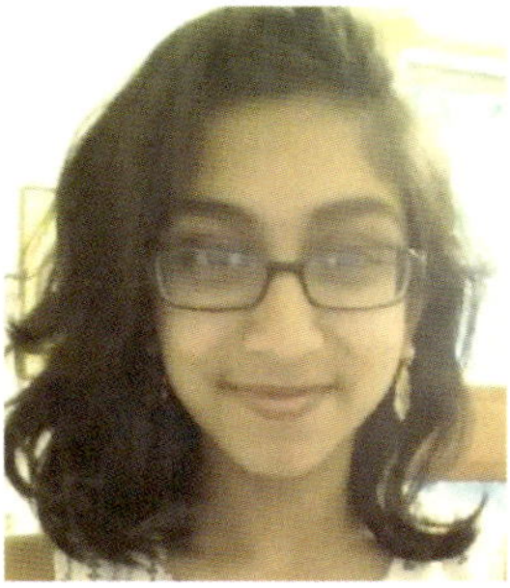

Shakira Morar won The 'Poetry for Peace 2016' Competition. This was part of the Arts Council funded collaboration between Jenny Lewis and Iraqi poet Adnan al-Sayegh (both featured in this collection) aimed at fostering greater understanding between English and Arabic-speaking communities. Adnan and Jenny worked with Oxford's Ashmolean Museum, the Foreign and Commonwealth Office, and the Poetry Society encouraging more than 60 11-to-17 year olds to produce poems for a competition on the themes of heritage and peace. The overall winning poem, chosen by Judith Palmer, Director of the Poetry Society, was *The Cracked Jug* (see p. 15).

DAVID OLSEN

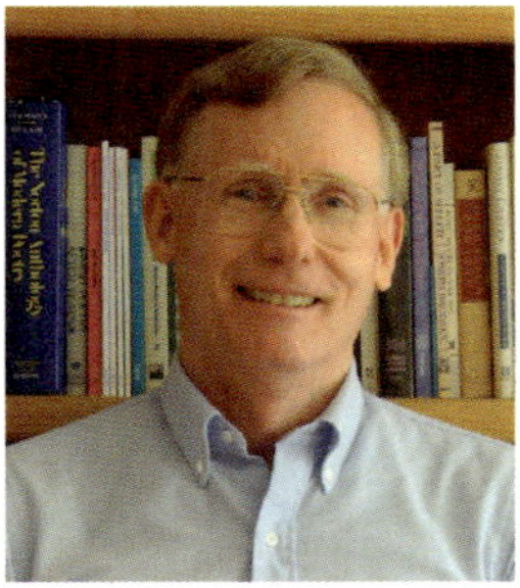

David Olsen's *Unfolding Origami* (80pp, 2015) won the Cinnamon Press Poetry Collection Award, and *Past Imperfect*, his second full-length poetry collection, is forthcoming from Cinnamon Press. His poetry chapbooks from US publishers are *Exit Wounds* (2017), *Sailing to Atlantis* (2013), *New World Elegies* (2011), and *Greatest Hits* (2001). David's poems have reached a wide audience in journals and anthologies produced in seven countries. A poet, fiction writer, and playwright with a BA in chemistry from University of California-Berkeley and an MA in creative writing from San Francisco State University, David was formerly an energy economist, management consultant, and performing arts critic. He has lived in Oxford since 2002.

HEATHER ROSSER

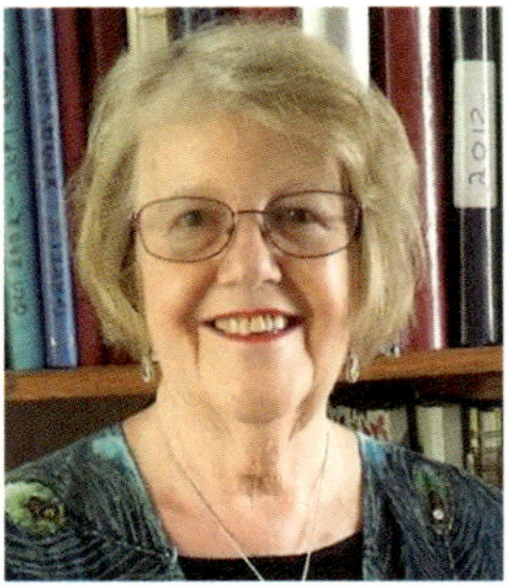

Heather spent 12 years in West Africa and Botswana working as a teacher, researcher, educational author and journalist. Since moving to Oxford she has written a series of social studies textbooks for primary schools in Africa and the Caribbean. *In the Line of Duty*, Heather's historical novel, is based on her grandfather's experiences as a seaplane pilot in the First World War. It was published by New Generation Publishing in 2014 and shortlisted for the Romantic Novelists' Association Joan Hessayon award in 2015. Heather has short stories published in *The Radcliffe Legacy, The Midnight Press* and *The Bodleian Murders* anthologies written by Oxford Writers Group and published by OxPens. Her website is www.heatherrosser.com

ADNAN AL-SAYEGH

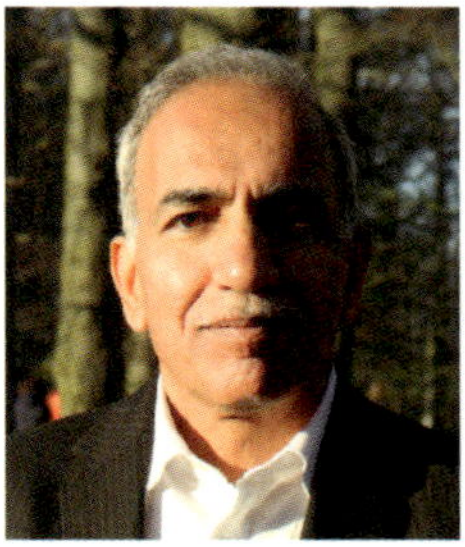

Adnan al-Sayegh was born in al Kufa, Iraq in 1955. His poem, *Uruk's Anthem*, is one of the longest ever written in Arabic literature (549 pages) and gives voice to the profound despair of the Iraqi experience. Adnan has published twelve books of poetry and his work has been translated into seven languages. His international awards include the Hellman-Hammet International Poetry Award (New York 1996), the Rotterdam International Poetry Award (1997) and the Swedish Writers Association Award (2005). Since 2004 he has been living in exile with his family in London.

SUDEEP SEN

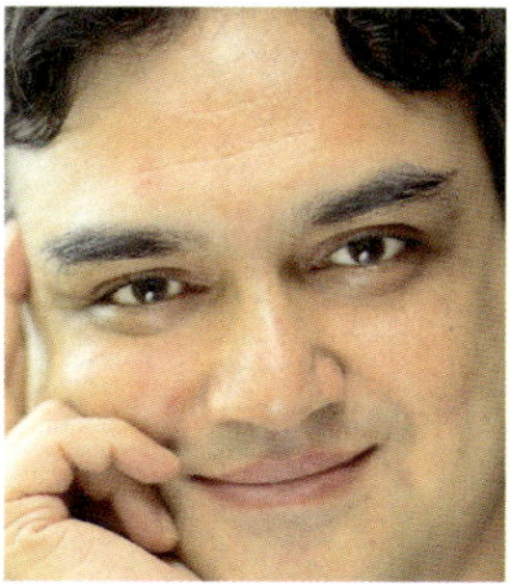

Sudeep Sen's prize-winning books include *Postmarked India: New & Selected Poems* (HarperCollins), *Rain, Aria* (A. K. Ramanujan Translation Award), *The HarperCollins Book of English Poetry* (editor), *Fractals: New & Selected Poems | Translations 1980–2015* (London Magazine Editions) and *EroText* (Vintage: Penguin Random House). *Blue Nude: New Poems & Ekphrasis* is forthcoming. Sen's works have been translated into over 25 languages. Sen is the editorial director of AARK ARTS the editor of *Atlas* and is the first Asian honoured to speak and read at the Nobel Laureate Festival. The Government of India awarded him the senior fellowship for 'outstanding persons in the field of culture / literature'.

SYLVIA VETTA

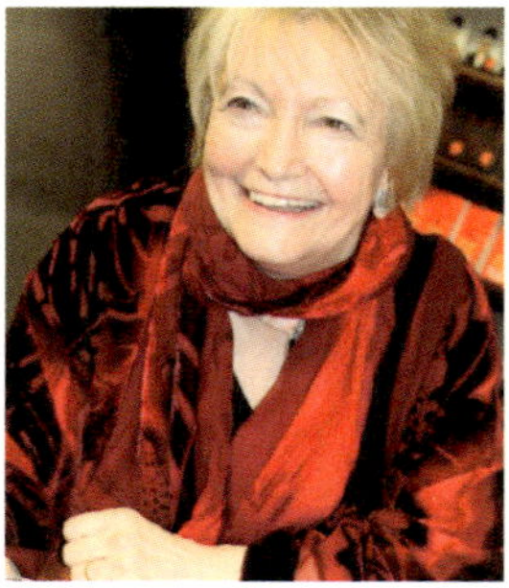

Sylvia is best known in Oxfordshire for her feature writing for *Oxfordshire Limited Edition* (1998–2017). She has written extensively about art, history and antiques for five magazines. 119 life stories of inspirational people with links to Oxford written by Sylvia were brought together in 3 books of *Oxford Castaways* (3, Oxfordfolio, 2017). Through her journalism Sylvia came to know the Manchurian born artist Weimin He (whose art is featured in this book). A poem she wrote inspired by him is on a hoarding in Jericho (Oxford). Her first novel *Brushstrokes in Time* set against real events in China (1963–1993) was published by Claret Press in 2016 and as an Audiobook by Essential Audiobooks (New York) www.sylviavetta.co.uk

NAZ PERVER WEICH

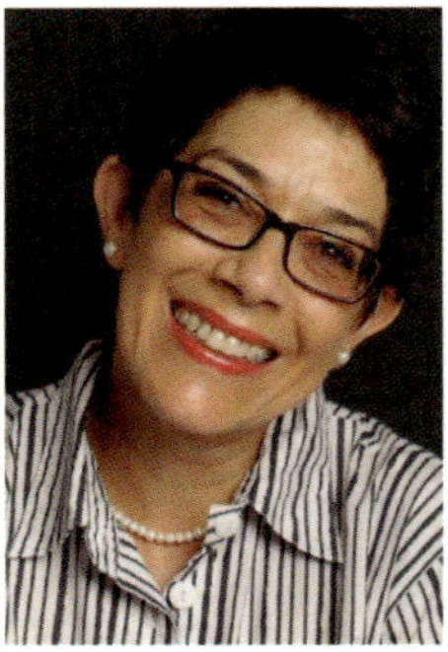

Born in Pakistan, Naz has lived in Italy, England, Germany, Pakistan, Canada and now Kenya. An avowed artist since her early teens, she won a scholarship to Italy where she studied at the Accademia di Belli Arti Pietro Vannucci in Perugia. She graduated in 1986 specializing in painting and photography. Naz has taken the influences of cubists like Picasso and Cezanne to inform and refine her own style. www.nazweich.com

WEIMIN HE

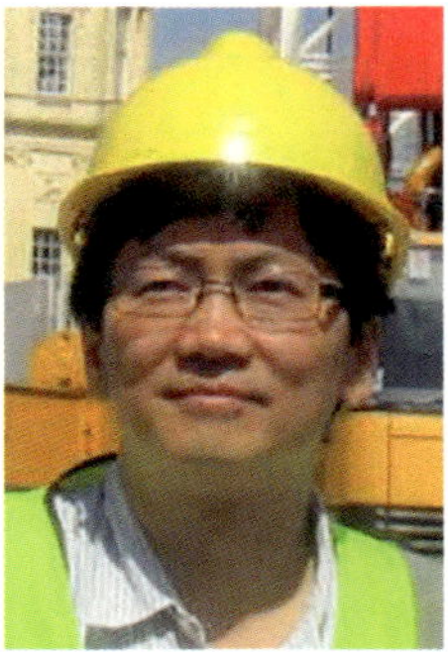

Manchurian born Weimin He studied painting and history of art in the Harbin Normal University and was awarded an MA in printmaking under Professor Quan Xianguang and Lu Tan at the Lu Xun Academy of Fine Arts in Shenyang Northeast. In 2005, he gained a PhD (Ulster University) and became the Christensen Fellow of Chinese Painting at the Ashmolean Museum. Following 6 years as artist-in-residence at the Oxford University Estates Services, in 2017, he had an exhibition in the Bodleian Weston Library and a book of his collected work in Oxford will be published in 2018. You will find his work in many public and private collections throughout the world including The British Museum and The China National Gallery. You can read his life story on the castaway blog on Sylvia Vetta's website and visit www.heweimin.org

STANDING VOICE : WHO WE ARE AND WHAT WE DO

BY THE STANDING VOICE TEAM

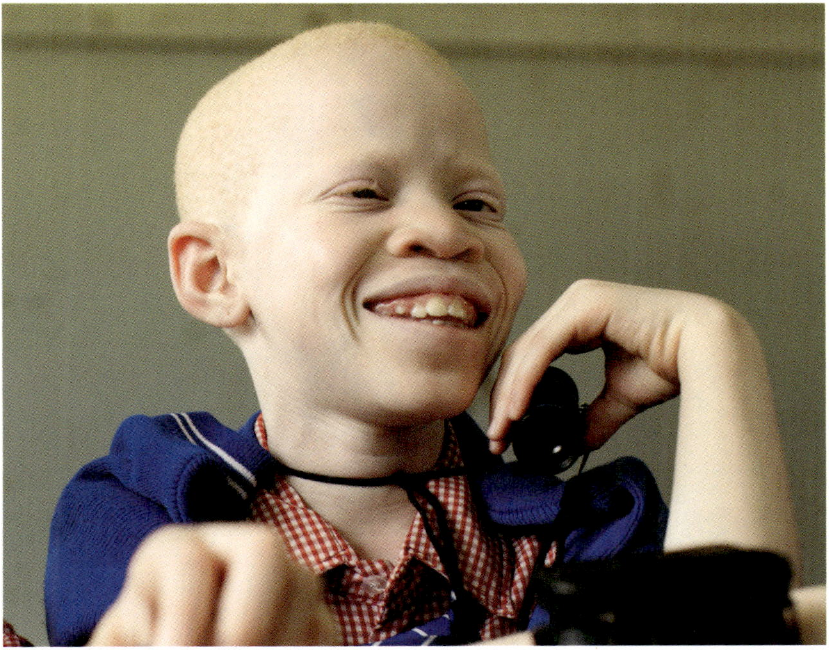

For people with albinism in Tanzania, persecution is a daily reality. Myths and misunderstanding enshroud albinism, transforming this rare genetic condition into a burden, a mystery, a curse. People with albinism lead lives blighted by stigma, shut out of civil participation and unable to access the most basic services. Violence, from school bullying to ritual killings, is commonplace: in Tanzania, there have been 64 documented attacks, and 76 murders, in the last ten years alone.

Standing Voice is a non-profit organisation working to make positive changes for people with albinism in Tanzania. We began as a documentary: a film conceived, shot and directed by Harry Freeland, our Founder. Over six years, Harry walked alongside people with albinism, seeing the world and its prejudice through their eyes. He met survivors of rape and abduction; siblings forced to eat from separate plates in the belief that albinism was contagious. These stories, pieced together from hundreds of hours of observational footage, became *In the Shadow of the Sun*, the ground breaking 2012 documentary that screened in 80 countries around the world.

Above all, the film was an effort to listen to people with albinism, and amplify their voices on a global stage. Today, listening remains the key principle of our work, driving everything we do. The people we help tell us that, after a lifetime of exclusion, what they want the most is to be accepted and embraced by their communities. For over ten years, this is what we have been striving to achieve. We empower people with albinism to take full—and fulfilling—roles in Tanzanian society, to let success be their greatest weapon against prejudice. When people with albinism are included, their rights are respected. Services improve; policies respond; communities heal.

On Ukerewe Island, we are proving just how successful this approach can be. Located in the heart of Lake Victoria, the island is home to a community we have worked alongside for more than a decade, and with whom we have built a compassion that transcends both genetics and geography. The hub of our work there is the Umoja Training Centre, constructed in 2015 as a space for community members with and without albinism to develop skills, establish businesses and form positive relationships. 'Umoja' in Swahili means unity, and, with the support of the whole community behind it, the centre has become an enduring symbol of the solidarity and understanding for which it is named.

However, prejudice is just one of a grinding series of obstacles that people with albinism face. The paleness of their skin leaves people with albinism at risk of developing skin cancer, especially in a hot country like Tanzania. In response, we have established a network of specialist clinics to provide dermatological care and education for people with albinism in their own communities. Because of our clinics, people are receiving sunscreen and learning how to protect their skin; lives are being saved. People with albinism also suffer from complex visual impairment. Left uncorrected, this can have debilitating consequences for their education and employment. Focusing on schools, here too we have created a programme providing specialist eye examinations and assistive devices for students with albinism, and training their teachers to understand their needs. This gives students the chance they deserve to succeed in their studies, and to grow as capable, confident individuals equipped to prosper.

We know first-hand the transformative power of small gestures, as simple as a pair of glasses. We are proud to have made these positive changes to the lives of countless individuals across East Africa. But in order to bring an end to prejudice, actions must be taken that reach beyond the individual, and even the national, level. That's why we are speaking out on international platforms, and seeking to raise the voices of people with albinism until they carry around the world. From the World Bank to the United Nations, our partnerships have empowered us to challenge the systems that make prejudice possible. Together, we can build the momentum of positive change, and amplify the voices of marginalised communities everywhere.

www.standingvoice.org

Standing Voice

www.standingvoice.org
info@standingvoice.org

/standingvoice

@StandingVoice

@standingvoiceuk

AN OXFORDFOLIO PUBLICATION

www.oxfordfolio.co.uk
oxfordfolio@gmail.com

/Oxfordfolio

@oxfordfolio